ORGANIZATION
SKILLS

ORGANIZATION
S K I L L S
by Richard Worth

A New England Publishing Associates Book

Printed in the United States of America
U-8

Library of Congress Cataloging-in-Publication Data

Worth, Richard.
    Organization skills / by Richard Worth.
        p. cm.
    Includes bibliographical references and index.
    Summary: Provides information about achieving efficient use of time
    on the job.
    ISBN 0-89434-211-8
    1. Time management. 2. Scheduling. [1. Time management.] I. Title
    HD69.T54W68   1998
    650.1—dc21   97-26627
                                           CIP
                                           AC

THE CAREER SKILLS LIBRARY

Communication Skills
By Richard Worth

Information Management
By Joseph Mackall

Leadership Skills
By Diane E. Rossiter

Learning the Ropes
By Sharon Naylor

Organization Skills
By Richard Worth

Problem-Solving
By Dandi Daley Mackall

Self-Development
By Dandi Daley Mackall

Teamwork Skills
By Dandi Daley Mackall

CONTENTS

I NTRODUCTION

All of us belong to organizations. Perhaps you are a member of a club or athletic team. You may have a part-time job in an organization, such as a fast-food restaurant or a clothing store. Your parents probably work in an organization, too. It may be a large company, like a manufacturing concern, or a much smaller firm, like a travel agency. Some organizations run very smoothly. They are tidy and efficient where everything usually is done promptly. Others are just the opposite. They are untidy and disorganized. Within them, nothing ever seems to be accomplished on time.

Individuals are the same way. Some of them always seem to be running late and never finish anything on schedule. Others are very well organized.

What is the main difference between a person with organization skills and someone who does not have them? It's the way they use time. Organized people do not waste it. This doesn't mean that they have to be working constantly. Organized people give themselves plenty of time for recreation or quiet reflection. But they also seem to get more tasks done—more short-term assignments and long-term projects.

If you want something done, give it to a busy person.

WORKPLACE CONTINUUM

Where would you place yourself
on this continuum?

DISORGANIZED   **WELL ORGANIZED**

There is an old saying that goes: "If you want something done, give it to a busy person." Well-organized people know how to fit a variety of projects into their schedules. They know how to get them done and how to do them successfully.

Today, employers are looking for people who can handle a number of different responsibilities. Like an accomplished juggler, workers must be able to keep several balls in the air at the same time and prevent them from falling. This takes organization skills. You can't wait to learn these skills on the job. Employers expect you to arrive there with them.

F A C T O I D

Since 1990, 30% of all workers have been laid off largely due to downsizings. Those that remain are expected to do more than ever before.

How do you develop organization skills? Many people begin learning them in school. They practice organizing important day-to-day tasks that need to be accomplished on time. These include homework assignments, extracurricular activities, and part-time jobs. Organization skills are relatively easy to master. They don't take hours and hours of practice, like playing the piano or perfecting a golf swing. But you must get into the habit of establishing regular routines for yourself and sticking to them.

You will find the rewards to be almost immediate—more control of your life, a greater sense of accomplishment, and a higher level of success. These are the benefits of organizing your time and using it to the utmost.

"Good order is the foundation of all good things."

—Edmund Burke

11

HOW WELL DO YOU MANAGE TIME?

1. Do you generally get up in the morning on time?

2. Do you usually have time for breakfast?

3. Do you catch the school bus in the morning?

4. Are you late for your first class?

5. Do you finish your homework assignments promptly?

6. Do you use study halls to complete tomorrow's work?

7. Are you on time for extracurricular activities?

8. Can you find papers in your desk or room at home?

9. Do you usually arrive at your part-time job late?

10. Do you complete assignments on your job promptly?

1 PLAN AHEAD

"**A**nd that concludes our training program," the instructor said, picking up her notes. "Oh, one more thing. Don't forget that each of you is making a presentation to top management Thursday morning. It's your chance to shine and show them what you learned. So be prepared!"

Bill rose and started to leave. "I'm glad that's over," he whispered to Evan. They had sat together during the entire program.

"Yeah, but there's still that presentation," Evan told him. "Mine's almost done. How are you doing?" "Oh, I'll get around to it," Bill answered confidently. "But not today."

Bill returned to his office and found a pile of telephone messages on his chair. It was almost 6:00 p.m. by the time he'd answered all the calls. As he looked at the clock, Bill realized that he was supposed to have a report on his boss's desk by the end of the day. He had had a week to do it. That seemed like so much time. Bill figured he could put it off. What a mistake!

He rushed around his office trying to gather all the figures for the report. Everything he needed wasn't there. But he couldn't help that now. Maybe his boss wouldn't notice. Bill typed away furiously for several hours. By the time he'd finished, it was almost midnight. He walked briskly into his boss's office and left the report on his desk. "Better late than never," Bill told himself.

The next day he was exhausted. But he had telephone calls to make all morning, a long sales meeting to attend, and a full afternoon catching up on paperwork. It was almost 6:30 by the time Bill finished. He was heading home, when his boss caught him at the elevator. "Look," he said, shaking his head, "this report you gave me is incomplete. You'll have to stay here tonight and rewrite it. I need it on my desk first thing in the morning."

Bill wanted to ask for a little more time, but he knew the report already was late and his boss was in no mood to listen to any excuses. Reluctantly, he walked back toward his office, passing Evan in the hallway. "See you tomorrow, Bill," he said. "Remember, eight o'clock sharp. We have to make our presentations."

Bill had completely forgotten. Now he had a report to finish *and* a talk to prepare for top management.

(Joe Duffy)

"Oh good, you're in early. We're ready for your report."

He slumped in his chair and started to work. Five hours later the report was finally complete, but Bill was completely worn out. "I'll just put my head on the desk for a few moments," he thought, figuring that a little rest was all he needed to tackle his presentation. The next time he looked at the clock it was 7 a.m.

15

(V. Harlow/Me & McGees Restaurant)

Being well organized is especially important in a fast-paced job where an employee must handle a number of different tasks at once.

TOO LITTLE TIME

Today, most people in the workplace have more to do and less time in which to do it. Many workers talk about always "running behind." Or they complain that there are "not enough hours in the day." Corporate downsizings have created more pressure on

16

everyone. As thousands of workers are laid off, those who remain are asked to take on greater responsibilities. One woman in the public relations department of a large manufacturing company has seen the staff cut by more than half. She's working longer hours and still has trouble getting everything done.

That's why time management skills are so important. If you procrastinate and don't organize your time very well, you'll end up the way Bill did.

FACTOID

In a recent poll, 50% of the workers surveyed said they are working longer hours than a year ago; 20% reported working two hours more each day.

Not only do employees have more to do, the nature of work has also changed. "Jobs aren't structured the way they used to be," explains human resources director Lisa Law. "Every job has more components to it. You can't specialize and you need to manage your time."

Not only do employees have more to do, the nature of work has also changed.

Law points out that in her company an accounts receivable clerk used to receive a bill, code it, and pass it on to someone else to check its accuracy. Now a clerk is expected to put the information from the bill on the computer, and check it himself. If the charges are incorrect, he must find out the reason and deal with it. What's more, all of this work must be completed within a tight deadline. "These things take time management and organization skills," Law says.

Because jobs are more complex, we must master more information to do them.

Because jobs are more complex, we must master more information to do them. Never before has so much information been available from so many sources. Books, magazines, television and the Internet provide us with enormous amounts of data. We need an opportunity to access it, evaluate it and figure out what to use. This puts even more pressure on us to use time effectively.

Yet we live in an age when everything seems to be moving so rapidly. And there never seems to be enough time. Fax machines and electronic mail (e-mail) enable us to communicate instantaneously. And the expectation is that we should do everything rapidly, packing as much as possible into each day.

According to a recent report in the *New York Times,* adolescents may be trying to do so much that they are not getting enough sleep. Classes, extracurricular activities, part-time jobs, and volunteer work are leaving students groggy and are affecting their grades. As Jan Farrington writes in *Career World* magazine, there is never enough time to do everything. "You

(V Harlow)

A well-organized work area enables this young office worker to locate the tools and papers he needs quickly and efficiently.

will always have to make choices about how you spend the time you have."

F A C T O I D

Adolescents need eight to nine hours of sleep each night. But a recent study says one-fourth of all teens sleep six hours or less.

EXERCISE

If we want to succeed in the workplace, all of us need to constantly learn new skills, so we can get more accomplished. Write about a new skill that you recently acquired on your job or in an extracurricular activity. How did you feel about being able to master this skill?

ORGANIZING YOUR TIME AND YOUR WORK

Time is not elastic. Each of us has the same amount of time each day—24 hours or 1440 minutes.

"If I only had a little more time." This statement is often heard from people who don't know how to use their time very efficiently. Time is not elastic. Each of us has the same amount of time each day—24 hours or 1440 minutes. It's how we organize this time that often determines how successful we will be. Of course, when some people hear the word "organize" they immediately start to groan. Who has time to get organized? Anyway, what's wrong with leaving things until the last minute? Always being late? Working in a messy, cluttered space? It's a chore to be organized.

Stephanie Winston, author of the best-selling book *Getting Organized*, disagrees.

"Organizing is fun, really," she says. What's more, it puts you "in charge of your world." As this book will show you, organizing your time and your work can bring you five key benefits:

1. You put first things first.
2. You learn to be on time.
3. You have more time.
4. You reduce stress.
5. You learn to be more selective.

You Put First Things First

Brian Beaudin is senior vice president for a business and industry association which sponsors programs in time management. One of the problems, as he sees it, is that employees often don't know which project should have the highest priority. "They start six things," he explains, "and don't finish any of them. They say, 'Oh, I think I'll start this letter.' Then they stop in the middle to make a phone call. Instead of going back to the letter, they say 'I have this report due,' and they begin the report. By the end of the day, nothing gets completed."

Effective time management ensures that this doesn't happen to you. It teaches you how to set priorities, how to determine which tasks are most important, and how to make sure those tasks get done. How critical are these skills on a job? A recent advertisement for an editorial assistant at a major publishing company sought candidates that have "the ability to work on and prioritize many projects at once." Thus, an editorial assistant is expected to keep many balls in the air at the same time and make sure none of them falls. This takes organization skills.

Melissa Gomez has a different type of job. She is an administrator at a small manufacturing company. Melissa describes her job as "organized chaos." But the emphasis is on the word "organized." Melissa is expected to write proposals for a variety of government jobs on which her company is bidding. Each proposal must be submitted by a specific deadline. If the proposal is late, her company will lose the project. Therefore, careful time management is essential.

Do not squander time, for that is the stuff life is made of.

—Benjamin Franklin

You Learn to be on Time

"In school you can be absent or late, and everything can be worked out," says career counselor Phyllis Garrison. "But the real world is different." Garrison says she gets feedback from employers that some students aren't responsible. The students don't "show up every day on time. Kids who are successful allow enough time for everything."

Adds college senior Rachel Anderson, "I think being on time is just an assumption that employers make. It's part of the job."

While still in high school, Anderson participated in a unique field study program. Students developed a list of businesses that might be interested in offering internships. They created a concise interview guide to determine what types of internships might be developed. Then they contacted the organizations, interviewed key individuals and analyzed the data. Finally, they wrote reports describing the internships, together with a plan to implement the program at their school.

"This project exercised the skills of time management," explains Charles Jett, who helped design it. "If you put off one step, then you can't proceed to the next one," he points out. Jett adds that if students left the task of collecting data until the last minute, then they wouldn't have enough time to analyze it properly or write an effective report. The moral is simple: Whenever you're involved in a team project, it's important to do each part of the project promptly. This takes time management skills.

EXERCISE

Describe the last time that you completed a project late or arrived late for something, such as a class or part-time job.

1. How did you feel about being late?
2. Did you offer an excuse for being late? If so, what was it?
3. What was the reaction of the person to whom you offered the excuse?
4. How did your tardiness affect other people?
5. Why is it important to be on time?

You Have More Time

Some people think that organizing activities takes too much time. But, in fact, it gives you more time. "You probably don't realize it," writes Jeffrey Mayer in his book *Time Management for Dummies,* "but most people waste almost an hour a day looking for papers that are lost on the top of their desks—60% of which they don't need anyway." (Chapter 5 describes how to make your work space more user-friendly so you can get more done in less time.)

By organizing your time, you're also more likely to remain focused on the most important things that have to be accomplished each day. This helps you avoid distractions. Once your priorities are accomplished, you have more time to relax.

FACTOID

In business as much as 50 to 70 % of the day is wasted on unimportant tasks like meeting with unexpected visitors and answering telephone calls.

You Reduce Stress

"Some people like living on the edge, but I don't," explains Anderson. "I find it very stressful to leave something until the last minute. I don't complete it as well." Anderson described a paper that she waited too long to begin. She needed time to finish a rough draft, put it away then go back to it in a few days to edit the paper effectively. But she didn't leave herself enough time. Then her computer broke down at the last minute and she had to scurry around to find another one. This just added to her stress.

Murphy's Law states: Anything that can go wrong will go wrong. And Murphy's Law invariably operates against you whenever something is left until the last minute. The computer breaks or the printer doesn't work. You wait until the last possible second to leave for a job interview, then you get stuck in traffic and arrive late. You decide to pull an "all-nighter" to finish that science project, then you come down with the flu and can't get out of bed.

Murphy's Law states: Anything that can go wrong will go wrong.

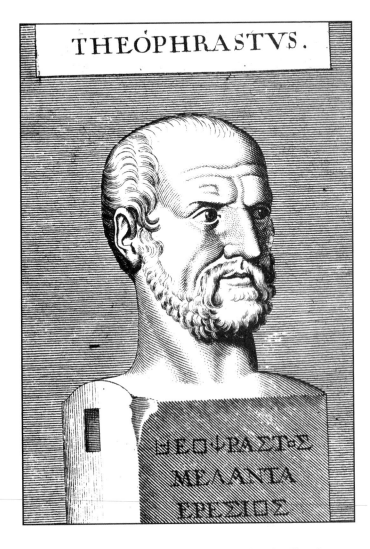

As long ago as the 3rd Century B.C., the Greek philosopher Theophrastus recognized the importance of time management. It's even more important in today's fast-paced world.

26

"We all know that running out of time puts us under stress," writes Alec Mackenzie, author of *The Time Trap.* "Decisions are made in haste and actions are taken under pressure....Effectiveness is diminished; deadlines are missed." By organizing your time, these problems often can be avoided.

You Learn to be More Selective

"Time management gives you an effective way of learning to say no," explains Jett. "You know you don't have time to do everything."

Peter Burns, a college senior, explains that he is involved in a variety of campus activities, perhaps too many activities. He works part-time, serves as president of his class, and tries to handle a full academic load. "I'd come home and there would be 15 messages on my answering machine," he explains. Burns says that he tries to get several important priorities accomplished each day but he never gets everything done. "I've had to be selective. I've begun to say no to opportunities. Academics are more important than extracurricular activities."

Time is the most valuable thing that a man can spend.

—Theophrastus, Greek philospher

(Courtesy: Prints & Photographs Division, Library of Congress)

With the increase of factories in the early 1800s, large number of employees had to be organized to manufacture products. Today, learning to work on a team can help you achieve your goals.

Time management is a way of giving yourself more control of your life. Instead of simply being reactive—responding to the messages on your answering machine or the requests of your friends—you can be proactive. Ask yourself: "What is most important to me?" The answer to this question can enable you to set priorities and establish goals.

In his book, *The 7 Habits of Highly Effective People,* Stephen Covey writes: "The challenge is not to manage time, but to manage ourselves." This means saying "no" to what is not important and saying "yes" to what is.

It's Time to Organize

Two centuries ago, farmers told time by the position of the sun. They organized their work by the seasons of the year—sowing in the spring, harvesting in the fall. If their schedule was off by a day or an hour, it didn't make too much difference. They just needed to do their work in the right season — this was the essence of time management for farmers. With the rise of the factory system, work changed. Large numbers of employees had to be organized to manufacture products. This meant that their work had to be timed precisely by the clock. All of them started their jobs at the same time, worked together as a team throughout the day and finished when the factory whistle blew. Thus, time management became an essential part of the workplace.

---

*"The most successful almanacs made time management their explicit focus, and of these [the]...*Old Farmer's Almanac, *by the middle of the nineteenth century had become the model for imitators all over the country."*
—Michael O'Malley, *Keeping Watch,*
    A History of American Time. (Penguin, 1990)

Today, it is even more important. Downsizings have reduced the number of employees in every organization. Those who remain are expected to do more work in the same amount of time. What's more, they are required to master not only one job, but often a variety of different jobs. Effective time management is a critical skill for anyone who wants to be successful. It enables you to focus on the important priorities, say yes to these things and make sure they are accomplished. It teaches you the value of being on time and reduces the stress associated with being late. Finally, spending a little time to organize your work can actually buy you more time.

The process of organizing your time and your life should begin now. In school or a part-time job, you have an opportunity to experiment—to learn what works for you and what doesn't. With this knowledge, you're far more likely to be an outstanding performer when you embark on a career.

EXERCISE

Do you organize your time and your life effectively? Answer true or false to the following statements.

1. I set priorities for myself each day. Each week. Each month.

2. At the end of each day, I generally feel that I accomplished something important.

3. I am easily distracted from doing my work.

4. I usually feel stressed out because I have too much to do.

5. I use a schedule that helps me plan my time.

6. I arrive late for appointments.

(Continued on page 32)

(Continued from page 31)

7. I keep my work space neat so I can find everything easily.

8. I clutter up my computer with unnecessary files.

9. I procrastinate and leave assignments until the last minute.

10. I often hand in projects late.

2 CHAPTER TWO
FIRST THINGS FIRST

Janet recently had joined her school's service club. Members of the club volunteered their time delivering hot meals to elderly shut-ins, staffing a hotline at the community crisis center and doing other types of service work. Each year, they also sponsored an auction to raise money for various community programs, such as a homeless shelter and a soup kitchen.

"As you all know," the president of the club began, "we're already receiving items to sell at the auction. But we have to make sure everybody in town knows about it. Since John Thompson graduated last year, there's no one to handle publicity. Are there any volunteers?"

As the club president asked this question, he was looking directly at Janet. She always had done well in English and even won a school writing prize. "How 'bout it, Janet, would you take on the job? You're the best qualified." She smiled and nodded her head.

"Thanks, it's very important," he said. "There are only two newspapers in town. Please find out their deadlines so you can be sure to get the stories in on time. We can't afford to be late."

Janet made a note on a small piece of paper and tucked it inside one of her notebooks. "I'll call as soon as I can," she thought. But that afternoon she had to go to her part-time job at the supermarket and forgot to contact the newspapers. As the days went by, Janet became involved in other activities. She had to finish her science project and study for final exams. There were applications to complete for college. About 10 days before the date of the auction, Janet sat down to write the articles for the local newspapers. It seemed like plenty of time. But as she opened one of her notebooks to jot down a few ideas, a little piece of paper fell out. It was the reminder to check the deadlines at the papers.

"Well, there's nothing I can do about it now," she thought. "I'll just finish these articles as fast as I can and get them into the papers." A couple of days later, Janet completed her final drafts and after school hurried down to one of the newspapers. She located the editorial office and gave the article to an editor. But as he looked at the date of the auction, he shook his head. "I'm sorry," he said, "our deadline for this type of article closed four days ago. You're too late."

Janet couldn't believe it. "But there must be something you can do," she said. "I'm afraid not," he told her, "there's just no room for it."

She left the office in a panic. She decided to call the other newspaper from a pay phone in the hallway. "The deadline has already passed," the editor told her. "But, maybe we can run a paragraph or two." "No one will ever see it," she shot back. "I'm sorry," he explained, "it's really the best we can do."

Janet hung up the telephone "How could I let this happen?" she said to herself. "What will I tell the other club members?"

WHAT IS QUALITY?

1. Eliminating mistakes.

2. Doing things right the first time.

3. Giving employers, customers, and teachers what they ask for.

BUSY...BUSY...BUSY

America's national pastime used to be baseball. Now, it's busyness. Whether at school or on the job, we

Being busy doesn't always mean that your most significant tasks are being accomplished.

seem to thrive on being busy. There are always projects to do, meetings to attend, assignments to complete, phone calls to answer, people to see, and e-mail to read. But being busy doesn't always mean that your most significant tasks are being accomplished. Take Janet, for example. She let a critical deadline slip, jeopardizing the success of the auction.

How often do you look back at the end of a week and ask yourself: Did I accomplish everything that was really important? Did I forget to do something that I should have done? Did I waste time on unimportant things?

FOUR KEY STEPS
IN ORGANIZING YOUR TIME

1. Determine how you spend your time now.
2. Make a "to-do" list.
3. Prioritize your activities.
4. Put those activities on a weekly schedule.

By organizing your time, you can avoid the type of problem that Janet encountered. And you can learn to use time more efficiently.

WHERE DOES THE TIME GO?

If you go to work in any major company today, you'll hear a great deal about "quality." Customers demand quality products. And major corporations have embarked on extensive programs aimed at improving the quality of their products and services.

How does a company know if it's making improvements? Quality control managers begin with what they call a "baseline." They look at the current numbers of defects in their products, like copy machines or automobiles. Then they set goals for improvement. After a certain length of time, they evaluate the company's progress to see if the goals are being met.

You can use a similar approach to improve the way you organize your time. Begin by looking at the way you use your time today. This is your baseline. By evaluating how your time currently is being spent, you may begin to realize why some of your most important projects are not being accomplished. Or, you may start to understand why you're always finishing them late.

37

EXERCISE

Keep a log for a week on how you use your time. This is your baseline. At the end of each day, write down:

	AMOUNT OF TIME
1. The amount of time you spend in class.	_____
2. The time you are in study halls and what you do with it.	_____
3. The time spent on extracurricular activities.	_____
4. The time spent talking on the telephone.	_____
5. The time spent watching television.	_____
6. The time devoted to homework assignments.	_____
7. The amount of time "hanging out" with friends.	_____
8. The time spent at a part-time job.	_____

MAKE A TO-DO LIST

"I make a to-do list, otherwise I forget things," explains career counselor Carol Peterson. "I have pads of paper in every room. As I think of things, I write them down. Then I put all of them on a central list."

If Janet had put the note to call the newspapers and check the deadlines on a central list, she might not have forgotten to do it.

Jose works for a small publishing company. Each week there are meetings to attend and important telephone calls to make. There are manuscripts to review, pictures to approve, and project reports to complete.

Unfortunately, Jose is chronically late for everything. It's not that he procrastinates; in fact, he is a very conscientious worker. But each time there is a new task for him to do, he writes it on a little slip of paper and puts it in some part of his office. His office is covered with these little notes. Often, one is tacked on top of another. Jose has no central to-do list with everything on it. As a result, calls go unanswered and he sometimes forgets important meetings.

Be sure there is at least one place where all the items can be found and checked off...keep it current and make sure it's available to you at all times.
— B. Eugene Griessman, *Time Tactics of Very Successful People*

At the beginning of each week, make a to-do list. What should you put on your list? If you're a student, you might include homework assignments that are due during the week, quizzes and tests, as well as club meetings. Suppose you work for the school newspaper. Your to-do list might include a staff meeting that you're expected to attend on Wednesday. In addition, you can use your to-do list to write down important errands, like picking up food and litter for your Siamese cat or remembering to rotate the tires on your car.

Sometimes you're given long-term assignments like a research paper or a science project. Instead of leaving them until the last minute, a much better approach is to break down each task into its logical steps. Then you can put each one on your to-do list and complete them, one after the other.

Break down each task into its logical steps.

High school counselor Angela Martinez tells students to "always write things down, otherwise they'll forget them. I tell college-bound students that professors won't plan for you. They'll just say that a paper is due on a specific date, and you have to create your own mini-deadlines for completing each part of it so you'll finish on time."

Perhaps you're assigned to write an article for the school newspaper that's due in three weeks. On your to-do list for the first week, you might put: "Conduct interviews and do research." For the next week, you might enter: "Write rough draft." And for the third week, you might write: "Revise rough draft and edit." By working backward from your deadline, you can determine what has to be accomplished each week to comfortably finish the task on time.

Suppose you've decided to obtain a part-time job. On your to-do list for the first week, you might put: "Write resume." For the second week you might assign yourself the task of identifying businesses in your area that could be looking for part-time employees. For the third week, you might decide to call those businesses and make appointments with the ones who want to interview you.

HALLMARKS OF AN EFFECTIVE TO-DO LIST

1. Keep only one list. Or if you start more than one, consolidate them onto one list every day.
2. Make the list neat and write everything so you can read it.
3. Post the list where you easily can see it.
4. Don't make the list, then ignore it. Use it to guide you.
5. Use the list for all your projects—long-term, short-term, and important personal goals.

Frequently, the days and weeks seem to be filled with projects that demand our immediate attention.

In his book, *The 7 Habits of Highly Effective People,* Stephen Covey points out that many of us seem to have very little time to focus on long-term goals. As a result, we can often miss out on unusual opportunities that may allow us to grow as individuals. But these things also belong on our to-do list—that's if we ever expect to fulfill our potential as unique human beings.

Julie worked for a large telemarketing firm. One day, she hoped to be part of management. In order to reach this goal, she knew that there were a number of steps she had to take along the way. There were training courses that she needed to attend in team building, communications, and leadership. She volunteered for special projects—projects that would expand her knowledge and develop her skills as a manager. Each week, Julie's work in her training courses and on special projects formed important elements of her to-do list.

EXERCISE

Make a to-do list for the week. Include short- and long-term assignments, errands, and extracurricular activities. Break down the long-term projects into separate steps and include the initial step on this week's to-do list. Make sure to also include an important goal you would like to achieve and the first step you might take toward realizing it.

SET YOUR PRIORITIES

Jamie is assistant manager of the human resources department at a small electronics firm. It's a two-person department, so she and her boss are busy constantly. Each week Jamie makes a to-do list of the tasks she wants to accomplish. Then, she breaks down the list day by day, establishing the top-priority items that she wants to have done by the end of each day. This is how Jamie insures that her highest priorities are always accomplished.

On Tuesday, for example, Jamie must finish preparing a presentation on the company's new health benefits program. She has to make this presentation to top management the following day. In addition, she wants to begin planning a summer internship program with a local community college. The college might provide two student interns to the firm each year. In addition, she wants to schedule a meeting with company supervisors to talk about sexual harassment guidelines for employees. Finally, she must finish the final draft of a new employee handbook. This has to be on the president's desk by Thursday morning. And Jamie has to be out of the office all day Wednesday so she won't have time to work on it.

Jamie believes that she can accomplish all of these tasks—that's if nothing unexpected occurs that demands her immediate attention. But in the workplace, crises often seem to occur when they're least expected. On Tuesday, the firm's receptionist walks into Jamie's office and suddenly announces that she is quitting.

Jamie spends over an hour talking to the woman, trying to convince her to stay on the job. But it's useless. Then Jamie meets with her boss, the human resources manager, and together they decide how to handle the situation. Jamie calls an employment agency that supplies temporary workers. The agency agrees to send over several job candidates who can fill the position for the short term. Jamie spends part of the afternoon interviewing three candidates. She also prepares a newspaper advertisement for another receptionist. She and her boss review the copy for the ad and send it to the newspaper.

By the time Jamie has finished handling the crisis, Tuesday has almost ended. None of her priorities has been accomplished. She can put off planning the new internship program and scheduling the meeting on sexual harassment guidelines. But the benefits presentation and the employment manual must be finished. Jamie stays late until both projects finally are complete.

Setting priorities is an important element of organizing your time and work

Setting priorities is an important element of organizing your time and work. This is the best way to insure that the most important items on your to-do list get done each day. Of course, no one has complete control over their time. Unexpected events are always occurring. And you have to adjust your day to deal with them. Perhaps you can put off some of your priorities, the way Jamie did. But others must be accomplished. If you set priorities, you can go back to them after a crisis has passed. And even if it means working late, you can accomplish your most important priorities every day.

William is a high school senior with a busy schedule. He has classes each day and homework, as well as a part-time job at the public library. Sunday night, before the week begins, he writes a to-do list. Then he selects the tasks that are his important priorities for each day of the week. William realizes that some of these priorities might change as he gets new assignments in school. Some of these assignments may become top priorities, and other tasks on his list may have to be postponed.

William's to-do list for Tuesday and the priorities he has set for himself are shown in Exhibit 1. His most important priorities have a (1) beside them, lesser priorities have a (2).

William must finish his English paper because it is due on Wednesday. He always has a math assignment. This

---

EXHIBIT 1.
William's To-Do List for Tuesday

Finish final draft of English paper	(1)
Start research for science project	(2)
Buy birthday gift for Dad	(2)
Do math homework	(1)
Meet friends at ice-skating rink	(2)
Work at library (4–6)	(1)

---

must be completed before the next class which is the following morning. He also has to work at the library. The other tasks are things he would like to do, but are not absolutely essential. His father's birthday, for example, is not until the following Monday, so he could postpone this task if necessary.

While William is sitting in history class on Tuesday, the teacher announces an unexpected quiz for the next day. This quiz now becomes one of his top priorities on the to-do list. To have time enough to study for the quiz and still complete the other essential tasks on his list, William may need to postpone all of his lesser priorities.

By prioritizing each day's projects, William is assured of accomplishing those that are most important—even if it means spending some extra time studying for a quiz.

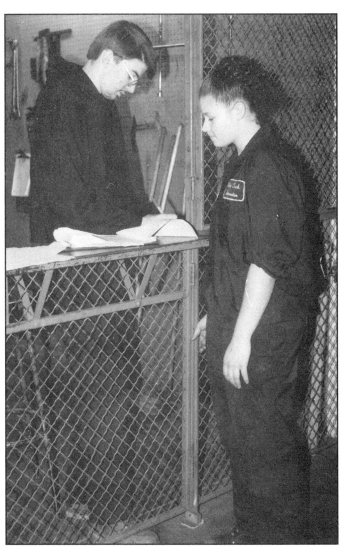

(V. Harlow/Vinal Regional Vocational Technical School, Middletown, CT)

To keep focused on your priorities, making a to-do list is essential. A to-do list will keep your life organized and help you meet deadlines.

EXERCISE

1. Return to your weekly to-do list. Break down the list into tasks that you want to accomplish each day. Place a (1) next to the most important priorities, place a (2) next to less important priorities.

2. Suppose your teacher gives you a new assignment on Tuesday that must be completed by the following day. How will this affect your list of priorities for that day? Suppose the car breaks down on Thursday while you're driving to work. How will this affect your priorities for that day?

DEVELOP A SCHEDULE

The fourth step in managing your time is to develop a weekly schedule, broken down day by day. "Some young people use planners," explains high school counselor Phyllis Garrison, "and this gives them a structured approach to everything."

A planner includes each day of the week, and it often divides the days into hours. First you can block out the time you spend in class. Then you can add the priority items from your to-do list. William's schedule for Tuesday is shown in Exhibit 2.

EXHIBIT 2
Williams Schedule for Tuesday

9:00–10:00 A.M.	English class
10:00–11:00 A.M.	Biology class
11:00–12:00 P.M.	Study hall: Start math homework
12:00–12:30 P.M.	Lunch
12:30–1:30 P.M.	History class
1:30–2:30 P.M.	Sociology class
2:30–3:30 P.M.	Meet friends at ice-skating rink
4:00–6:00 P.M.	Work at library
6:30–7:00 P.M.	Dinner
7:30–9:00 P.M.	Finish English paper
9:30–10:30 P.M.	Start science project

William has four hours of classes on Monday. If you recall, his math homework was a top priority, so he schedules it for his study hall at 11:00. William had hoped to meet some friends at the ice-skating rink, but his history teacher announced an unexpected quiz for the following day. Therefore, he decided to stay at school and complete his math homework so he would have time at night to study for the quiz. On his schedule, William includes two other important priorities: working at the library and finishing his English paper. He also had hoped to start his science project. But he had to change his schedule and study for the history quiz instead.

Although William's schedule is busy, he still leaves himself sufficient time between various activities. "Some students don't leave themselves enough time to get from one place to another," says Peterson, "like getting from school to a part-time job." William allows half an hour, more than enough time, to drive to and from his job at the library. He also builds in free time during the evening to take breaks. Breaks are an important part of any schedule. You can use them to have a snack, watch television, or call friends. Breaks give you a chance to refresh yourself so you can do your work more effectively.

EXERCISE

Create a weekly schedule, broken down day by day. Use the information from your to-do list and your daily list of priorities. Block out your classes. Include any extracurricular activities or part-time jobs. Be sure to leave enough time for travel and breaks.

MANAGING YOUR WAY TO SUCCESS

Managing your time and your work is a step-by-step process. It begins by taking stock of where you are now. Ask yourself: How do I currently spend my time? How many of my important priorities are really being accomplished? Would I be more successful in school and in the rest of my life if I spent my time differently?

Make yourself a to-do list at the beginning of each week. Every day, as new projects come along, add them to your list. We rarely have time to do everything on our to-do list. So it's essential to set some priorities for yourself and decide the most important things you must do every day. Finally, make a schedule that enables you to carry out the high-priority tasks on your list. You'll be delighted to discover how much more productive you become.

"People are always blaming their circumstances for what they are. I don't believe in circumstances. The people who get on in this world are the people who get up and look for the circumstances they want, and, if they can't find them, make them."

—George Bernard Shaw

51

MY "TO DO" LIST

My goal this week is to: _____

Task	Priority	Deadline	Completed

3 CHAPTER THREE
ELIMINATING TIME WASTERS

Michelle was supposed to be studying for a science test. It was an important exam which counted heavily toward her final grade. But she just couldn't seem to get down to work.

First, there was a telephone call from her friend Arlene, complaining about her boss again. "I don't know what to do," Arlene began. "My boss is so unfair. He doesn't care about anybody." Forty-five minutes later Arlene finally stopped talking and Michelle hung up the telephone.

But she had no sooner gone back to studying for the test, when the doorbell rang. It was her friend Karen from up the street. "You'll never believe what happened," she told Michelle. Karen had the latest gossip about their friends Bill and Carol who had just broken up. It took her at least an hour and two cups of coffee to pour out the entire story. Then it was time for Michelle's favorite television program, so Karen stayed to watch it with her. By the time she left, it was 10 p.m.

"I've really got to start studying," Michelle told herself. But first she decided to check her e-mail.

There was a short letter from her brother who was away at college. She decided to answer it.

Finally, Michelle opened her chemistry notes. She looked at the clock—11 p.m. The exam was scheduled for first period the next morning and Michelle hadn't even begun preparing for it.

TERRIBLE TIME WASTERS

Michelle is no different from many of us. She wants to get her work done. Indeed, she even may have reserved a large block of time in her schedule to study for the chemistry test. But somehow she finds herself getting distracted by interruptions. After all, what's more enjoyable? Talking to your friends or reviewing your science notes?

Learn to say no like a maniac to your time wasters.

—**Helen Gurley Brown,**
Editor, *Cosmopolitan*

Unfortunately, time wasters prevent you from completing your most essential priorities. Whether it's a school assignment or a project on the job, you can't afford to let a critical task go undone because of unimportant distractions.

The telephone can be one of your biggest distractions. Unless you learn to control the phone, it will surely master you. Why? There is something about the insistent "ring-ring" of the telephone that seems to demand our attention. Whenever we hear that sound, our tendency is to stop whatever we're doing—no matter how necessary it may be—and immediately answer the call. We simply must find out what the caller has to say to us, even if it means interrupting something else. So, we pick up the telephone and put the rest of our schedule on hold.

Telephone messages generally fall into three categories: essential, time-limited, and unimportant calls.

Essential Calls

Essential calls require your immediate attention. These might include a call from your boss who needs to discuss a critical presentation that you're making at tomorrow's sales conference. Or perhaps you receive a call from a customer who wants you to find out why a shipment is late. Essential calls are ones you must answer and spend as much time as it takes to handle them properly.

FACTOID:
The average business call lasts six minutes but could have been concluded in two minutes—a third of the time.

Time-Limit Calls

Time-limit calls may be important, but they should be handled as quickly and efficiently as possible. For example, a member of your work team may call with a specific question about a report you're working on together. You answer it in about a minute. Then he spends the next 20 minutes talking about his recent vacation. This is a real time waster that can delay high-priority work. It's essential to put a limit on these calls. Otherwise you'll find yourself frittering away precious minutes. If your coworker wants to talk about his vacation and you have a project to accomplish, you don't have to cut him off rudely. Explain the situation as pleasantly as possible: "I'm sorry, but I really have to get this done. Can I call you back later or see you for lunch? I'd love to hear about your vacation." Make an appointment to call him, if necessary, and mark it down on your schedule.

Unimportant Calls

These calls are unimportant compared to the work you really need to accomplish. Michelle's call from Arlene falls into this category. She should have been studying instead of spending 45 minutes listening to Arlene's complaints about her boss. But perhaps Michelle is one of those people who simply has trouble saying "no." She's afraid of offending her friends, so Michelle finds herself listening to their telephone monologues. What else could she do?

One high school senior interviewed for this book explains that when she's involved in an important assignment, she simply tells friends who call that she will have to speak to them later. She is nice, but firm. This senior seems to have no trouble saying "no" or dealing with her high-priority tasks *before* she spends time on the telephone.

If saying "no" is more of a problem for you, perhaps you should consider a telephone answering machine. This is an effective way to screen calls and decide whether you want to answer them. In business, the answering machine is often called "voice mail." It's important to have a message that's short, friendly, and encourages callers to talk. For example, you might say: "I'm sorry I can't take your call right now. But, after the beep, please leave a message. I'll get back to you as soon as I can." In this way, you won't miss their message but you won't be forced to tell them "no" when they want to talk to you.

Surprisingly, you'll also find that many of your calls do not have to be returned. Frequently, a caller is just providing you with information that requires no response. Perhaps a customer is calling to say he can't

Frequently, a caller is just providing you with information that requires no response.

make tomorrow's luncheon appointment or a co-worker is leaving you some statistical data. This type of message usually does not require a return call from you.

You might also consider using e-mail as a way of avoiding interruptions while doing homework. Suggest that friends use the Internet and send you letters by e-mail. At various intervals throughout the evening, take a break from homework to check your e-mail. If anything seems very important, answer the e-mail and send the responses to your friends.

FACTOID:

Approximately 50% of all telephone calls are simply conveying information that requires no response.

EXERCISE

Telephone calls can be terrible time wasters. Keep a log of your calls for a week. Mark each call:
- *Essential*
- *Time-Limit*
- *Unimportant.*

Indicate how much time you spend on each call. Finally, decide what steps you could have taken to cut down your telephone time.

(V. Harlow/Me & McGees Restaurant)

While you are at work, remember that business comes ahead of your personal life. Taking care of customers should be your first priority. Personal business should be done on your own time.

TALK...TALK...TALK

It used to be that the water cooler was the symbol of corporate America. Newspaper and magazine cartoons showed employees standing around the water cooler trading the latest gossip. Not any more. With corporate downsizings, there are far fewer employees in every organization. That means everyone has more work to do and there's very little time to stand

With corporate downsizings, there are far fewer employees in every organization.

around the water cooler and talk. What's more, any employees seen wasting time this way are apt to find themselves looking for new jobs. Teyonda Riley works after school at a fast-food restaurant. She knows that the restaurant manager expects her to be standing behind the cash register waiting on customers all the time that she's there. If her friends come in and want to talk, Teyonda makes it clear that she has no time to spend with them. "Business comes first," she says.

TYPES OF TIME WASTERS

- ▶ Needless telephone conversations
- ▶ Useless chit-chat
- ▶ Unnecessary interruptions by coworkers
- ▶ Poor planning in doing errands

When you're trying to get work done, management experts suggest that you prioritize conversations just as you do telephone calls. Some are essential, others are unimportant, and still others must be time limited. Career counselor Carol Peterson must juggle a variety of tasks in her job. She calls employers, trying to find part-time jobs for students. She talks to the students themselves, helping them with resumes, job searches, and interviewing strategies.

Peterson's conversations with students are *essential,* because they depend on her for information. The conversations Teyonda Riley described are *unimportant* so she wisely avoids them. But you probably will find that many of your conversations at work are *time limited.* And it's necessary to learn how to handle them or you won't get your high-priority tasks accomplished.

One approach is to politely answer brief questions, but put off more complicated ones until later when you have more time. Suppose you're in the midst of an important project, and a coworker stops to ask you a question. "We just received a shipment from Acme Lighting. Do you know where the shipping order is?" If you know the answer, you can stop and quickly answer the question.

But suppose your coworker wants to continue the discussion. "You know, I've been meaning to mention something. I think we need to improve our order forms." At this point, you realize that the topic might lead to a long conversation that will interrupt your work. You might say: "I'm sorry. I know this may be important to you. But I can't stop right now. Why don't I call you later and we can talk about it then."

This enables you to have a brief conversation, without taking very much time away from your project.

Another way of dealing with the same situation is to suggest that your co-worker speak to someone else about the new order forms. You can point out that this person might be more knowledgeable on the subject than you are. Finally, you might encourage your co-worker to do some research on his own. He could find out what kinds of forms other companies use, and perhaps even design one of his own. Then he might come back and talk about it.

Each of these approaches enables you to set a time limit on conversations and keep yourself focused on the important work that has to be done each day.

HOW DO YOU KNOW IF A CONVERSATION IS ESSENTIAL?

▶ It involves an emergency that can't wait.

▶ It involves your boss who must speak to you immediately.

▶ It involves the school principal who wants you in her office.

▶ It involves a friend or family member who is depending on you for help.

▶ It involves a coworker who can't complete a project without some essential information that you possess.

EXERCISE

Keep track of those conversations that occur during the day which distract you from your work. How many of them were unimportant? How many could have been much shorter? How could you shorten them?

MORE TIME WASTERS

Linda saved Saturdays to do her errands. She made a mental list of what she had to accomplish and set out to get everything done. But she always complained that she never had enough time.

Lets look at Linda's typical Saturday. She drives to one part of town to drop off her dry cleaning. Then she retraces her route to shop at a children's clothing store near her house. Linda wants to buy a birthday gift for her one-year-old niece. No sooner has she completed this purchase, than Linda realizes that she needs to go to the bank to deposit her paycheck. But it's next door to the cleaners. So she drives over there again.

By now, it's lunch time and Linda returns home. During lunch she realizes that she has forgotten something else on her shopping trip—a birthday card to go with the present for her niece. The card shop is only a block from the children's clothing store, so after lunch she retraces her steps to that part of town. Then Linda has to do some grocery shopping. Guess what? The supermarket is next to the bank. By the end of the day, Linda feels thoroughly exhausted.

Many people waste time because they don't plan their activities very effectively. Keeping a mental list of what you need to do may not be enough—it's too easy to forget something. Instead, write out a list of your errands. Then group those that are in the same geographical area and do them together. This way, you're not spending a lot of needless time driving around.

Smart salespeople use a similar approach when they make calls on customers. A salesperson doesn't make one visit, return to the office, go out again and see another customer in the same area, then return back to the office. This wastes too much time. Instead she calls ahead, sets up appointments and tries to see all her customers in the same area on the same day. This cuts down the amount of time she has to spend in traffic.

> **Many people waste time because they don't plan their activities very effectively.**

EXERCISE

Make a list of the errands you have to do this weekend. Group those errands that you can do at the same time and in the same physical area. How much time do you save by doing these errands together?

USING SMALL BLOCKS OF TIME

Most of us are forced to spend some time each day traveling to and from work or school. We're also likely to get stuck in traffic. Teacher Anna Gonzalez has learned how to put this time to good use. "My drive to work really makes me think about my day," she says. "I make a note of any important telephone calls I need to make at school. Otherwise I forget them or put them off. I also think about any obligation—like a meeting I have to prepare for—and write it down."

Make the most of downtime and in-between time.

—B. Eugene Griessman,
Time Tactics of Very Successful People

Little blocks of time can be especially valuable if you know how to use them. If you ride to school on the bus in the morning, you can use the time to quickly review your notes before a first-period test. A bus ride to your part-time job is another chance to get some work done—like a brief reading assignment.

Busy managers know how to use their downtime efficiently. If they travel and their plane is delayed, they bring work to the airport and do it while they're waiting. During this downtime, they might write a letter, read a report or make telephone calls to customers. A doctor's appointment is another occasion when downtime can be used effectively. Instead of sitting in the waiting room doing nothing, this time can be used to do some work.

EXERCISE

When do you accomplish your best work? During the next week, keep track of the times when you have the most energy. Is it early in the morning? During the middle of the day? Late afternoon? Evening? Schedule your most difficult tasks during these periods.

WHEN DO YOU WORK AT YOUR VERY BEST?

Each of us has a time of day when we feel freshest and have the most pep. For Anna Gonzalez, that time is the morning. "I have more energy then. That's when I like to schedule important appointments—like meetings with my principal."

Some of us are "morning" people. That's the time when we do our best work. If you're one of these early birds, schedule your hardest tasks—those that take the most thought—for the morning. Carol Peterson says that she performs at her peak during two times of the day—early morning and early evening. "I do the hardest things, then." College senior Peter Burns explains, "I get my best work done after 11 P.M. I know that by getting things done then, I won't feel miserable the next morning."

By contrast, time management experts suggest that you should do less demanding tasks when you have the least amount of energy. In his article, "Time, for a Change," published by *Men's Health*, Richard Laliburte points out that the period between 4 and 5 P.M. is the least productive part of the work day. Therefore, he recommends that this time be reserved for simple tasks, such as cleaning up your work space.

TIME WAITS FOR NO ONE

No one can slow down the passing of time. But you can exercise more control over it and increase what you accomplish each day. One way of getting more done is to eliminate those little time wasters. These include some of the lengthy telephone calls and face-to-face conversations that can keep you from doing your work. You can also use time better by designing your schedule to take advantage of your peak energy periods and your down time, and by arranging your errands so they can be done most efficiently. These seem like little changes. But you'll be surprised at the difference they can make in your life.

CHAPTER FOUR
THE PITFALLS OF PROCRASTINATION

Gerry Saunders was a video producer. He created presentations for large companies that they used to sell their new products—anything from baby clothes to cat food. Gerry was considered very talented. Indeed, one of his videos recently had won an award for special effects. Although Gerry was a top-flight producer, he suffered from a terrible problem—procrastination. He always put things off until the last minute.

"I like working on the edge," he said. "It gets my creative juices flowing." But Gerry's procrastination drove his employees to distraction. "One of these days, you're going to cut it too close," his assistant told him.

"Stop worrying," Gerry reassured her. "When have I ever missed a deadline?"

Gerry was currently working on a video presentation for his most important client—a well-known toy manufacturer. They were introducing a new computer game at their annual sales conference. The video was the highlight of the conference, and it was scheduled to be shown at 10 A.M. on the final day, just before the conference ended.

Once again, Gerry left everything until the last minute. The client, Bill Fitzgerald, asked to see a rough cut of the video a couple of days in advance. Gerry promised to give it to him. But he never delivered. "I really wanted to see the video before we showed it," Bill explained.

"I'm sorry," Gerry said. "But everything will be all right. Trust me."

"I guess I have no choice," Bill told him.

With only one day to go before the conference, Gerry worked furiously to finish the videotape. On the last night he never went to bed, and finally at 9 a.m.—an hour before show time—the video was complete. Gerry was very proud of what he'd accomplished.

"It's the best thing we've ever done," he told his assistant. She nodded her head wearily. "Now you've got to get it to the client." Gerry jumped in his car with a copy of the tape and started driving across town to reach the conference by the deadline. Unfortunately, he hadn't counted on traffic. A huge truck had jackknifed on the highway, and cars were backed up for five miles.

There was no way Gerry would reach the conference on time. The deadline came and went. The videotape was never shown.

(Joe Duffy)

When Gerry finally arrived, he saw Bill sitting alone at one end of the auditorium. Everyone else already had gone. "I'm terribly sorry," Gerry began. "I tried. I really tried. I did the best I could."

"No you didn't," Bill said angrily. "You always leave everything to the last minute. This time you made me look like a fool. Now I'm going to do what I should have done a long time ago—find another producer. Gerry, you're fired!"

WHY DO PEOPLE PROCRASTINATE?

It's easy to put things off. Suppose you receive an assignment to write a paper. The deadline is several weeks away. "Don't worry," you say to yourself. "There's plenty of time. I can start the assignment later." So you forget about it. Time goes by and you become involved in other things. One day you remember to look at the calendar. You can't believe it. Suddenly, that deadline is only three days away. And you have to work furiously to get your paper done. "Where did the time go?" you ask yourself. Procrastination often seems to make time move more rapidly. By putting off projects, the deadlines appear to sneak up on you almost before you know it.

Procrastination often seems to make time move more rapidly.

Why do people procrastinate? Some say they enjoy "living on the edge," like Gerry Saunders. They just can't focus on a project until the deadline is almost on them. Then they work nonstop—around the clock, if necessary—until the task is accomplished. Some people claim to do their best work that way. But even if they don't, leaving everything until the last minute gives them a convenient excuse. If the project doesn't

72

turn out quite as well as they wanted, they can always say, "Well, I ran out of time." It's an easy way to let themselves off the hook.

PROCRASTINATORS' EXCUSES

▶ "I can always put it off until tomorrow."

▶ "I do my best work when I'm up against a deadline."

▶ "I've got more important things to do now."

▶ "I'm not a procrastinator, I just don't like rushing into anything."

▶ "If I put it off, maybe the project will go away."

▶ "If I don't do it, perhaps my boss will forget about it."

▶ "I want to stop procrastinating, but I don't have time."

▶ "There's so much to do, I don't know where to start."

▶ "I don't want to get started too soon."

▶ "I'll get it done, just don't push me."

"More plans go astray...more time is wasted by procrastination than by any other single factor," explain Merrill and Donna Douglass in their book *Manage Your Time, Manage Your Work, Manage Yourself.* Most of us fall back on procrastination to put off those unpleasant tasks—the ones we really don't want to do. Instead of starting your math homework, you decide to watch a half hour of television. Then you call a couple of friends on the telephone. Late in the evening, you finally get around to your homework. By that time, you're tired, so you complete only part of it and go to bed.

Sometimes a task may seem so difficult or overwhelming, you don't want to begin. So you put it off. Karen's boss asked her to take some special computer training. But she was afraid the courses might prove too hard for her. Whenever her boss would stop by Karen's desk and inquire if she'd enrolled in the courses, she would say, "Oh, I'll get around to it." But she was afraid to enroll. Karen's fears caused her to procrastinate. But without the necessary training she might eventually lose her job.

Most of us feel anxious when we have to try something new and unfamiliar. But procrastination is no solution to that problem. Indeed, putting things off may only make them seem worse than they really are.

Sometimes a task may seem so difficult or overwhelming, you don't want to begin.

EXERCISE

Are you a procrastinator? If you answer "yes" to two or more of these statements, you probably are.

1. I regularly put off unpleasant projects and concentrate on doing what I enjoy.

2. I often feel overwhelmed by a new, unfamiliar assignment and put off starting it.

3. I can usually find a reason for not getting down to my work.

4. I'm easily distracted from my work by interruptions.

5. I always seem to run out of time and never finish a project by the deadline.

6. I enjoy living "on the edge" and leaving assignments until the last minute.

7. Friends and coworkers often tell me I should start projects sooner.

DEALING WITH PROCRASTINATION

It was Howard's senior year in college. He knew it was time to start making plans for his life after graduation. Some of his friends already were lining up jobs at large companies. Howard's parents had already warned him that he would have to support himself once college was over. But Howard was having such a good time on campus, he didn't want to think about next year. Anyway, the entire process of looking for a job seemed so overwhelming, he just couldn't face it.

When you're dragging your feet on a task that seems endless or insurmountable, break it down into simpler components.
—Stephanie Winston,
The Organized Executive

How can Howard start to deal with this situation and conquer the problem of procrastination? The best approach is to take it one step at a time. Otherwise, it's easy to feel overwhelmed. Howard might begin slowly, by having a conversation with his college career counselor. Perhaps they could explore areas that might be interesting to him. Then Howard could try an internship in one of these areas. By working part-time as an intern, he can find out if he really likes the work. The internship also gives him valuable hands-on experience that can prove very appealing to an employer when Howard looks for a full-time job after graduation.

As a next step, Howard might attend various career fairs and talk to companies that are hiring recent college graduates. This experience might help him target several prospective employers. Finally, he might send out his resume and a cover letter to each of these companies and arrange employment interviews.

By breaking down the process into small steps, Howard can accomplish all of them—one by one. In this way, job hunting won't seem so overwhelming. He can put each step on his schedule for specific times throughout the year. Then he can accomplish them without putting off the job-hunting process until the last minute. By that time, it is likely to be too late. The opportunities for internships will have passed. The job fairs will be over. And Howard will find himself far less likely to find a job that appeals to him.

Many people feel overwhelmed by a long writing project, like the task of completing a term paper. They look at a blank computer screen and say to themselves, "How am I going to write so many pages?" If you approach the task that way, you can easily defeat yourself before you start. But that's not the best way to begin. Instead, you tackle the term paper section by section. Each section has to be only a few pages long. You set a deadline for yourself and finish each section by the deadline. Perhaps you even break each section up into several parts, spending a few hours every day on each one. And before you know it, you've completed an entire section. Then you begin thinking about the next section, and write it the same way. The term paper seems far less daunting if you break it up into small pieces. You're much less likely to have a panic attack this way than if you try to think about writing the whole project at once.

Breaking a large project into tiny, bite-size pieces is an effective method of beating procrastination. Once,

---

WAYS TO STOP PROCRASTINATING

1. Don't try to change yourself overnight, start slowly.

2. Begin with a small project—one you've been putting off.

3. Finish the project ahead of schedule.

4. Take time to enjoy the satisfaction of getting the job done.

5. Buy yourself a small present as a reward.

6. Now try a larger project.

Rachel Anderson, a college senior, worked part-time at a coffee and bagel shop. Her responsibilities included making sandwiches, cleaning up the store at the end of the day, and setting up for the next morning. It was a demanding job that clearly had no place for procrastination. Rachel had to break down some of the tasks into manageable pieces in order to get them all done. Then she scheduled these tasks for various times throughout the day.

For example, Rachel was given a half hour to close up the shop. In order to get everything done on time, she would put away the tablecloths after customers had finished eating in the afternoon. Once she had finished with the sandwich boards at lunch and would no longer need them, she would immediately clean the boards and put them away. Rachel would also bring up the cleaning supplies early so they would be ready when she had to mop up the floor. By completing tasks step by step and not leaving them until the last minute, she had plenty of time to get everything done.

The tendency to do things we like, rather than the things we ought to do, is almost universal.

—Alec Mackenzie, *The Time Trap*

The following sections describe several other tips that will help you beat the pitfalls of procrastination.

Don't Put Off an Unpleasant Task

Suppose you're late shipping an order, and you have to call an unhappy customer. This is never a pleasant task. And no one wants to do it. But putting it off doesn't make it any easier. Indeed, if you spend the entire day anticipating that call, it will only seem worse. Instead, do it early in the day. This is often the time when you're fresher and you have the most energy. Then, it will probably be easier to get the task accomplished.

Reward Yourself

After you complete an unpleasant task, give yourself a pat on the back. Do something enjoyable. Take a break or have a snack. Make a telephone call to a friend and chat for a few minutes. This is a good way to put the unpleasantness behind you and get on with the rest of your day.

Take Action

Sometimes a task seems so complex, it's hard to know where to start. In this type of situation, it's easy to become immobilized and do nothing. You keep putting off the project, procrastinating, until the deadline is finally staring you in the face. Then you panic and do a poor job.

Sometimes you have to approach a new task by using trial and error. Suppose your boss wants you to come up with a new form for ordering supplies. "This isn't my job," you say to yourself. "Why did he ask me?" But your boss isn't the type of person who likes to be questioned when he makes a decision. First, you try not to think about the project. Maybe he'll change his mind and forget it. But as the days go by, he keeps asking you about the new form. How do you deal with this type of problem?

Finally, you realize that you have to start somewhere. So you talk to people at your company who deal with suppliers and ask for their advice. Little by little you gather information. Some of it is useful; some isn't. You experiment with several new designs for the form. And eventually, by trial and error, you figure out an approach that may satisfy your boss and create the new form.

Keep Your Priorities Straight

If you make something a top priority, chances are you'll get it done. Constantly review your to-do list for the day and the week. Look at your schedule. Determine your top priorities and stay focused on them. This will enable you to get the most important items accomplished.

EXERCISE

If you're a procrastinator, now is the time to change your habits. If you have a lengthy task, break it down into bite-size pieces. Then put each piece on your weekly schedule.

If a task seems complicated, take action and start somewhere. Deal with an unpleasant task early in the day, instead of putting it off. And make sure to stay focused on your priorities.

Keep a log for the next month. Use the tips discussed in this section. Are you completing tasks sooner and more efficiently? Do you complete more of them before the deadlines?

ARE YOU A PERFECTIONIST?

By his own admission, Darryl was a perfectionist. He was always looking for just the right line to start a report. And he wouldn't begin until he found it. As a result, he often procrastinated. He'd put off a report until the last minute and frequently miss a deadline completely. Darryl also failed to prioritize things very effectively.

For example, he would often put as much energy into writing an e-mail to one of his coworkers as he did into an important memo to his boss. From his point of view, both had to be perfect. Darryl would spend hours and hours at his desk going over his written work until it was absolutely flawless. Long after everyone else had left, he was still there.

"Perfection can't be expected in this world."

—Old Proverb

The search for perfection often turns very responsible people into procrastinators. It also prevents them from prioritizing their work successfully. Some tasks simply don't need to be done perfectly, like Darryl's e-mail. Others demand a much a higher standard, like Darryl's memo to his boss. If you try to make everything perfect, you'll end up driving yourself crazy. What's more, you're apt to put in needless hours of work that could be spent on something more important.

If you're like Darryl, you can deal with this problem by using the same approach discussed in chapter 3.

Evaluate your tasks according to the three criteria: essential, time limited, unimportant. The essential tasks require the highest standards of excellence and usually the most time. But even these may never reach perfection. If you're a perfectionist, start by putting less pressure on yourself. Accept a little less. You'll be much happier.

HOW TO DEAL WITH PERFECTIONISM

1. Realize that people won't think any less of you because you're not perfect—they aren't perfect either.

2. Recognize that nothing is ever perfect, it can always be improved.

3. Be kind to yourself, accept a little less than perfection.

4. Don't give a project more than the time it really deserves.

5. Reward yourself for a job well done.

YOU DON'T HAVE TO BE A PROCRASTINATOR

"I used to be a procrastinator," admits Carol Peterson. "I stopped. I felt overwhelmed and hated that feeling." You can stop being a procrastinator, too. First, accept the fact that the projects you're putting off aren't going to go away. By worrying about them, they'll often seem harder. And by leaving them until the last minute, you often won't get them done as successfully.

Instead, you'll use your time much more effectively if you work on ways to overcome procrastination. Don't let large projects overcome you. Divide them into manageable parts. Treat unpleasant projects just like you would a swim in cold water—jump right in; it's often easier to get it over with as quickly as possible. And if perfectionism is causing you to procrastinate, settle for a little lower standard.

Don't let large projects overcome you. Divide them into manageable parts.

"There is no more miserable human being than one in whom nothing is habitual but indecision."

—William James

As one writer put it: "Procrastination is the art of keeping up with yesterday." This is another way of saying it always makes you feel as if you're behind. If you want to get ahead, eliminate procrastination.

5 WHERE YOU WORK *DOES* MAKE A DIFFERENCE

"**C**arol, how do you ever find anything in here?" Jim asked, as they sipped their coffee together in her tiny office.

"I can't help it if I'm not a neat freak like you are," she smiled. "I've got other priorities." Throughout the company, Carol's office was generally referred to as "the pit." There was paper lying everywhere. It was falling off the window sills. Files bulging with paper were stacked on the chairs. Tall paper skyscrapers rose from the floor. And Carol's desk was covered with papers, leaving barely an inch of space on which she could do her work.

"I'll clean it up someday," she kept telling herself. But "someday" never came. Indeed, the mess in her office grew worse and worse. What Carol didn't seem to realize was that she wasted precious time hunting for important files that were hidden away under stacks of paper. Since she was never quite sure where

(V. Harlow)

A cluttered, disorganized work area slows down productivity and adds stress to your job.

the files might be—or, for that matter, if they were even in her office at all—it made the task of locating them very stressful. The additional stress made her job much more difficult than it had to be.

One morning Carol was sitting behind an enormous pile of papers on her desk. She was putting the final touches on her segment of an important presentation—a presentation she and her work team had to make to their boss, the vice president for manufacturing. "Are you almost ready," Jim asked, sticking his head inside Carol's office. "We're due to go on in less than half an hour."

"Yes, I'm all set," she answered. Jim came over to her desk and together they looked over the material she had prepared. Suddenly, he noticed that something was missing.

"Where are those figures you received from the Department of Commerce in Washington?" he asked. "We can't make this presentation without them." Frantically, Carol and Jim went through everything in the folder, but the figures weren't there.

"I know they're here somewhere," Carol said. Jim looked around the office. "How will we ever find them in this mess?" he asked. "Come on!" she pleaded. "They've got to be here. Help me look." Carol began digging through the stacks of paper on her desk, desperately searching for the missing figures. Meanwhile Jim attacked the files on the window sill. Then he started looking through the piles of paper on the floor.

WORKPLACE CONTINUUM

Where do you fall on this continuum?

MESSY   **NEAT**

Finally, he shook his head. "It's no use," he sighed. "We don't have any more time." Carol was very upset. "How could I do this? The whole team was counting on me and I let them down."

NEATNESS COUNTS

Some people like working in a messy environment. They seem to thrive in chaos. Perhaps they're fortunate enough to have a willing assistant—someone who keeps them on track, ensures that they make most of their deadlines on time and prevents them from drowning under a pile of paperwork. But you're not likely to have such a person in school or on your first job. It's completely up to you to keep yourself organized.

F A C T O I D :

Employees spend as much as one hour each day searching for papers on their desks.

Perhaps you're one of those people who convinces themselves that they can always find what they need amid the clutter in their work space. Sometimes you can, but frequently it happens only after a lengthy search. More often than not, you aren't so lucky and lose something important, just the way Carol did.

How do you deal with this problem? The first step is to make a note on your to-do list. In big letters, write: CLEAN UP WORK SPACE. Make it a top priority. Put it on your schedule. And set aside enough time to get it done. As you clean up the books and papers strewn around your work area, you may even discover at least one or two items you thought were lost forever. Perhaps you'll find a treasured piece of jewelry that slipped under a pile of papers, or a prized pen that rolled underneath some books. Getting organized can have a lot of benefits.

This doesn't mean that you have to suddenly become a neat freak. You don't need to clean off every space, arrange all your files in a row or carefully align all the books in your bookcase. While some people may like this type of order, it isn't necessary for successfully managing your projects. What will help, however, is an effective method of organizing your materials so you can find them quickly and work with them as easily as possible.

The best way to tame the paper tiger is to develop a simple filing system.

A SIMPLE FILING SYSTEM

The best way to tame the paper tiger is to develop a simple filing system. You might begin by organizing the papers in your work space according to three categories: *essential, lower priority,* and *unimportant.*

Essential papers deal with projects that you're currently working on—those assignments with the highest priority. Each of these should be given its own file folder. And the name of the assignment should be carefully marked on it. For example, "Civil War Report," might be the title of one folder. Then you can keep all the papers relating to that project inside the folder. Since this is an essential, high-priority project, that folder probably should remain on your desk.

Some people rely on an "in-box" to help them with their filing system. Attorney Karen Jeffers uses a three-tiered box. On the top level are her "pending" files and papers. These refer to essential, high-priority projects that she is currently working on. Pending matters also appear on Karen's to-do list for the week. On the second level are projects that have lower priority. They don't have to be done immediately. She puts the deadlines for these projects on her calendar to ensure that they will eventually be accomplished. But the deadlines aren't immediate. These projects might be handled next week or next month. On the lowest level of the in-box are papers marked "to the file." These refer to unimportant matters. Perhaps they are projects which have already been handled.

Instead of leaving these papers out to clutter up her office, Jeffers regularly puts them away in her filing cabinet. Every file in these cabinets is carefully marked according to the specific project. Then any papers relating to that project can be placed in the appropriate file.

F A C T O I D :
Less than half of the paper that finds its way to your desk on the job is worth your attention.

There is one final category of paper—*trash.* "If you don't need a paper any longer put it in the recycling bin or throw it away," explains author Jeffrey Mayer. Much of the paper we receive every day is useless. Yet we often seem reluctant to get rid of it. Take mail, for example. A great deal of it consists of catalogs or other kinds

Much of the paper we receive every day is useless.

of junk mail, trying to persuade us to buy something. How many of these products are you ever likely to purchase? Yet the letters and catalogs often hang around week after week, because we never get around to throwing them away.

Perhaps you receive letters from friends. Some should be answered immediately. Others may need no answer at all. But after a certain length of time, most letters don't have to be kept around any longer. They simply fill up your work area and should be discarded. You may also find yourself keeping papers and research materials from old projects completed months ago. Most of these may have little or no value. They simply take up space. By throwing them out, you can reduce the clutter in your work space enormously.

EXERCISE

If your work area is filled with papers and files, now is the time to start bringing some order to this chaos. Organize the material according to the three-category system: essential, lower priority, unimportant. Then add the fourth category—trash. Use the "1 in 20" rule. If you haven't looked at the item once in the last 20 days, put it in a file cabinet or throw it out.

TOO MANY NOTES

Tom's office looked like a woodland in autumn. There was a forest of little colored notes—pink, yellow, green and orange—pasted everywhere. They were hanging on the walls, bookcases, desk and file cabinet. They contained telephone numbers, reminders to do something or important statistics for a report. Unfortunately, there were too many notes in too many places. And Tom usually forgot to look at any of them. Or, if he did need to find a specific note, he had to search the entire room before locating it.

Bringing order to your notes is just as important as organizing your files. Some notes can probably be thrown in the wastebasket because you no longer need them. Others may relate to a particular project that's already completed. They can be put in the appropriate folder for that project inside your file cabinet. Other notes may refer to priority projects that you are currently handling. These should be placed in the appropriate files in your in-box. Of course, there are always a few notes that relate to very significant matters for which you have no file. These might include a telephone number for someone you met recently and plan to call for lunch. This type of note might be put on a small corkboard near your desk so you can refer to it easily.

Bringing order to your notes is just as important as organizing your files.

95

HALLMARKS OF CLUTTER CHAMPIONS

1. The floors in their rooms never see the light of day because they're covered with books and dirty clothes.

2. Their desks look like dumping grounds for old papers.

3. Their trash baskets are overflowing and haven't been emptied in weeks.

4. Their computers are filled with loads of unnecessary files that they no longer use.

5. Their offices are piled high with stacks of unfinished projects.

6. Their to-do lists and weekly schedules are never updated because no one can find them.

7. Their notes are pasted up everywhere and no one looks at them.

When it comes to organizing notes and papers, the one guideline you should always remember is: BE

SELECTIVE. There isn't room to keep everything out in front of you. Some of it may belong on your desk. Some belong in the file cabinet. And the rest probably should be thrown away.

The same rule applies to files on your computer. People often fill up their hard drive with useless files that they no longer need. Many of these can be deleted. Others can be transferred to disks and stored in small filing cabinets on your book shelf. This leaves your hard drive available for the really important items.

...if we had time to organize, we'd be less harried. But if we were less harried, we'd have time to organize.
—Richard Laliburte, writer

ORGANIZE WHAT YOU READ

In the workplace, information comes at us from everywhere. Some of it is valuable. But much of it isn't. How do you keep your work space from becoming a large storage closet, filled with piles of magazines and newspapers? Once again, you have to learn to be selective and keep only the material that you need.

Some people maintain an article file. They clip magazine and newspaper articles that may relate to their projects and place all of them in a single file. They throw away the papers and magazines. While this cuts down on the clutter in their offices, it may create another problem. After a short period of time, the file is bulging with all types of articles. And to find one relating to a specific subject requires looking through the entire file.

One freelance book writer uses a different approach. He creates a file for each book that he's writing. Every time he sees an article relating to the book's subject, he clips the article and puts it in the appropriate file. He may work on each chapter of the book several weeks or even months apart—in between working on other projects. But when he eventually starts writing, the article he needs is right there in the file.

EXERCISE

As you are assigned writing projects in school, begin to clip articles from newspapers and magazines that relate to these projects. Start a file for each project. Put the articles into the appropriate files, so they'll be there when you need them.

A HOME OFFICE

Sandy's company needed to save some money. They decided to close the regional sales office where Sandy and her colleagues worked. All of the employees were asked to work out of offices at home. Sandy had mixed feelings about working at home. She liked the freedom it provided. But she was concerned whether she'd have the discipline necessary to actually get all her tasks done each day.

FACTOID:

One survey showed that almost three-fourths of employees feel they are more productive when working at home than in an office.

Many people feel the way Sandy does, although more and more of them are working from home. Some of these people set the same schedules for themselves that they would keep in an office. They start work at eight or nine o'clock in the morning, take a break for lunch, and continue working until five or six in the evening. This helps them avoid the temptation of staying in bed late, or taking the afternoon off and not completing all of their work. They also try to avoid the distractions that were discussed in chapter 3. They don't allow themselves to waste

99

much time on unimportant telephone calls. If a friend drops over for a chat, they keep these conversations limited.

THE WORST DISTRACTIONS WHEN YOU WORK AT HOME

▶ A sunny day that lures you outside.

▶ A refrigerator filled with good things to eat.

▶ Your favorite daytime television programs running back to back.

▶ A telephone call from your best friend, who never stops talking.

▶ A new computer game you just bought yourself.

▶ A chat room on the Internet where you can talk to people about your hobbies.

People with home offices also try to create a work space for themselves that is entirely user-friendly. Are you a person who likes to look outside while you work?

Then you need to put your office in a room with a window. Select a sturdy desk for yourself and a comfortable chair. Make sure the important items are easy to reach, like the telephone, computer, or fax machine.

You'll also need an in-box and a handy file cabinet to take care of your files. Some people like to keep little organizers on their desks to organize important items like paper clips, pens, rubber bands, and tape. A desk calendar is essential to maintain your schedule, and a corkboard to post a few notes.

EXERCISE

Many of the same items you need for a home office are also necessary for the space where you do your homework. Do you have all of them?

► Sturdy desk
► Comfortable chair
► Strong light source
► Handy file cabinet
► Desk calendar
► Organizer for paper clips, pens, rubber bands, tape, etc.
► Corkboard
► In-box

"Start by doing what's necessary; then do what's possible; and suddenly you are doing the impossible."

—St. Francis of Assisi

KEEP YOUR WORK AREA ORGANIZED

Organizing your workplace will increase your efficiency and enable you to accomplish more in less time. The key to organizing paper is learning how to be selective. This means keeping only the highest priority items on your desk. Unimportant items that you no longer need should be thrown out.

The rest can be put in your filing cabinet. A good filing system is essential because it will help you find notes and articles when you need them. It will also enable you to keep piles of paper from growing all over your work area.

Finally, the work space itself should be user-friendly, so you'll want to spend time there doing your projects. Remember, where you work *does* make a difference—a difference that can lead to greater success.

You may wish to put out one or two personal photographs, showing you with your friends or members of your family. You might also decide to display

(V. Harlow)

A well-organized filing system keeps important papers in their place so they are easy to locate when the need arises.

a small award which you won in school. But don't get carried away and display large posters or calendars. They may look tacky. Indeed, your company may have a policy against hanging these things in your office.

CHAPTER SIX
SEVEN SECRETS OF BETTER TIME MANAGEMENT

It was almost midnight and Sharon was still studying. "If I can only get through these last few pages of notes, I know I'll get an A on that test," she thought as her eyes started to close.

By her own admission, Sharon was an intensely focused student. She kept to a very rigorous schedule, with little time for anything else but work. For example, every night she regularly spent three to four hours on her homework. Sharon set very high standards for herself, accepting nothing less than the best. Or, perhaps it would be more accurate to say that her parents would accept nothing less from her. They expected her to get into a top-rated college. And after graduation, Sharon's father expected that she would follow in his footsteps and become a doctor.

To be accepted at a prestigious college, Sharon not only had to excel in academics, she also had to participate in various extracurricular activities. As sports editor of the school newspaper, she covered varsity games and wrote up detailed articles on them. She was also captain of the school debate team. Both activities were extremely time consuming. When she wasn't studying, Sharon was preparing for a debate or putting the finishing touches on an article about a recent basketball game.

Sharon seemed to be working constantly. "It's the price you have to pay for success," her parents told her. "And we want you to be successful." Was this the way Sharon wanted to go through high school—working herself sometimes to the point of exhaustion? She never really asked herself that question. She didn't have time.

Step 1: Leave Time for Personal Goals that Are More Important to You

American employees are more productive today than at any time in the past.

Many people seem to put heavy demands on themselves. Surveys tell us that American employees are more productive today than at any time in the past. We no sooner complete one task than we start another. Indeed, many people admit to trying to do several things at the same time. They read the newspaper, eat breakfast, and watch television. Or they talk on the telephone, write a grocery list, and surf the Internet.

(Joe Duffy)

In the 19th century, the French writer Alexis de Tocqueville observed that Americans always seemed to be in a hurry. Nothing has changed. We seem intent on cramming as much as possible into every day. But very few of us stop to ask whether these are the things we really want to be doing, whether they really satisfy our personal goals.

A good schedule can help us organize the tasks we do each day, but it cannot tell us what those tasks ought to be. We have to make those decisions ourselves. If you're planning to attend college and embark on a satisfying career, you'll need to study hard, just the way Sharon did. But make sure you also leave time for yourself. Build in time for quiet reflection, evaluate what you're doing, and ask yourself whether you're on the right track. Perhaps Sharon was happy with her busy schedule. On the other hand, she may have wanted to spend more time doing something else. Don't let your schedule get so rigid that you can't allow yourself an opportunity to change. Suppose Sharon wanted to learn to play a musical instrument or just spend more time hanging out with her friends. This may have taken time away from another activity—time she may have been afraid to give up for fear of disappointing her parents. It's easy to let time slip away and find yourself carrying out someone else's priorities. As you organize your days and weeks, set aside enough hours to do what you think is important.

Time wasted is existence; used, is life.

—**Edward Young,**
18th-century English poet

> **EXERCISE**
>
> What is the most important personal goal that you would like to achieve? What steps have you taken to attain it? What else could you be doing to reach this objective?

Step 2: Don't Overschedule Yourself

"I overschedule myself and then feel badly if I don't get everything done," explains career counselor Carol Peterson. Indeed, many people try to take on so much that there aren't enough hours in a day to handle all of it.

According to a study by Professor Roger Buehler and his colleagues, people regularly underestimate how long it will take to actually complete a project and therefore don't leave enough time for it. The study showed that the subjects' time estimates may have been off by as much as three weeks for long-term projects, like a senior thesis. And they may have underestimated the time for a shorter project, like repairing an automobile, by as much as three days.

Buehler points out that the same problems exist on the job. Employees tend to be overly optimistic about the time it will take to get something done.

They overschedule themselves, promise too much, and don't leave enough time to get their projects accomplished.

One way to deal with this problem is to recall similar tasks that you had to do in the past. For example, what kinds of obstacles did you face in writing a report for your supervisor? Did it take you longer to collect all the necessary research data than you thought it would? Did you need to obtain information from coworkers who were out of town and unavailable? Thinking about all the hurdles that had to be overcome in the past may be enough to persuade you to build in some extra time when undertaking a similar project.

As you estimate the amount of time to do a project, don't forget to build in another 10 % for Murphy's Law. This law states: Anything that can go wrong will go wrong. A computer glitch, for example, can wreak havoc with any schedule. A traffic jam can make you late for an appointment, unless you've allowed yourself some extra time to get there.

Expect the unexpected, then be prepared to deal with it. Jim had carefully prepared a slide show to present to new employees as part of their orientation program. As he flipped on the projector, the light bulb blew out. Unfortunately, a spare bulb wasn't readily available and the entire presentation had to be postponed. Jim was embarrassed and he made a negative impression on the new employees. Once again, Murphy's Law had claimed a victim.

People who are well organized have learned how to prepare for the unexpected. This means not only building in extra time to deal with unanticipated problems, it also means using some of that time to prevent them from turning into disasters. Bulbs often have a way of blowing out when you turn on a slide projector to present your first slide. Jim should have taken a few moments to round up an extra light bulb in advance of the presentation. This just takes a little planning.

EXERCISE

1. Do you try to schedule too many things in too little time? If so, how does it make you feel? What could you do to schedule yourself more successfully?

2. Recall a situation when you were working on a project and something happened that threw off your entire schedule. How did you cope with it?

Step 3: Do It Right the First Time

Betsy prided herself on an ability to finish projects faster than anyone else. She had a knack for organizing information quickly. This meant she could turn out memos and proposals very rapidly. Unfortunately, she didn't spend quite enough time checking all her facts. Nor did she proofread her work very carefully to eliminate grammatical errors. As a result, Betsy's supervisor sometimes had to send the material back to her for corrections before sending it out to his boss—the vice president for operations.

Betsy may have finished a proposal very quickly, but by the time it went up to her supervisor and came back to her again for corrections, the project actually took longer than if she had done it right the first time. Betsy's mistakes also undermined her credibility in the eyes of her boss.

American companies recognize the importance of producing quality products.

American companies recognize the importance of producing quality products. This means making them right the first time—without any defects that need to be repaired. If they want to keep a customer coming back, companies realize that they must build products, like computers, automobiles, and dishwashers that run effectively. They also know that it costs less in time and money to make a product right the first time rather than go back and repair it.

The same principle applies when you do your work. It's far less time consuming to do it right the first time, than to go back and do it over and over again. It also earns you far higher marks with your supervisor.

Many of us seem to put too much emphasis on speed, just the way Betsy did. Somehow, faster always seems to be better. But if you try to complete a task too quickly, you're apt to make mistakes—mistakes that will cost you time and energy later. Slow down and build a little extra time into your schedule to review your work and revise it if necessary. This will enable you to submit a much better finished product.

EXERCISE

Think of a project that you tried to complete too fast. What was the result? How did you feel about it? If you're working on a project now, what can you do to avoid needless mistakes in it?

Step 4; Put Your Schedule in Writing and Make It Specific

Jenny recognized the importance of having a schedule. But she could never bring herself to write one down. "I'll just keep it in my head," she thought. "I can remember everything that way." Unfortunately, there were too many things for her to remember. Take yearbook meetings, for example. She'd often forget about them. And sometimes her assignments were late, because she neglected to write the due date on her calendar.

In order to organize your time effectively, don't trust your memory. You must write everything down. As soon as you receive an assignment, put it on your to-do list. Look at the other things you have to accomplish and determine whether this new assignment should be given a higher priority. Perhaps something else on your to-do list can wait and just as easily be done later. Bump this project to another day and replace it with the new one that has a more important priority. Then give this higher priority project the time slot on your schedule that had previously been filled by the lower priority item.

If your schedule is shifting regularly and you need to handle a variety of projects, you must be as specific about them as possible. Suppose you're working on several assignments for your supervisor. With the hectic schedule that you must maintain at your office, you realize that it will be necessary to work on at least one of these projects at home. So you make a note on your schedule for Thursday night: "Work on project."

Thursday arrives and you look at your schedule. You put the project notes in your briefcase and head for home. Unfortunately, you picked up the notes for the wrong project. This one has a much lower priority than the one you're suppose to be doing. So you must go back to the office and pick up the notes, wasting precious time.

That's why it is so important to make your schedule specific. When you made up the schedule at the beginning of the week, it may have seemed obvious which project you were going to do on Thursday. But by the time Thursday arrives, you have forgotten it. Why depend on your memory when it's so easy to write down everything? A few extra seconds spent making your schedule specific can save you far more time later on.

EXERCISE

Look at your schedule for the week. How specific have you been in writing down each assignment? If an assignment is to be done three or four days from now, will you clearly understand what you're supposed to do by the time you get to it?

Step 5: Have a Place for Everything

Disorganized people constantly seem to be looking for things they can't find. Perhaps it's an important paper that's disappeared from their files. Or it may be a vital telephone number that suddenly seems to be missing just when they need it most. If you're one of these people, you should select some convenient places to put materials and routinely store them there. Then, you're likely to find the information when it's needed.

As explained earlier, high-priority files might be placed in your in-box and less important ones in your file cabinet. If you're finished working on a file, don't leave it out in your work space. It might get lost. Return it to your in-box or your file cabinet. Return papers to the appropriate file after you've finished with them. Otherwise they may be lost or misplaced.

When it comes to telephone numbers, some people like to keep them on little slips of paper strewn around their work area. But this is a sure-fire way of losing them. A much more organized approach is to keep a book of telephone numbers, and put important new ones in there soon after you receive them. Another handy place to store telephone numbers is on your computer. Many systems have a built-in program for recording names, numbers, and addresses.

It's also a good idea to keep supplies in a convenient location near your desk so they're easily accessible. Instead of hunting around the room for paper clips, scissors, or pens, always keep them in the same place. Use a desk organizer. And always put the items back after you use them. This way you don't have to search for them later when you need them again.

EXERCISE

Look at your work space and go through a mental checklist. Are your files carefully organized? Are important telephone numbers easy to reach? Are your supplies handy? Is your desk neat enough to get your work done?

Step 6: Practice Self-Discipline

Organized people use a disciplined approach to getting things done. Exhibit 3 presents the key elements of self-discipline by comparing a self-disciplined person to one who is not.

EXHIBIT 3. THE KEY ELEMENTS OF SELF-DISCIPLINE

Self-disciplined	**Unself-disciplined**
Works on projects in the order of their priority.	Deals with projects haphazardly and in no particular priority.
Routinely completes assignments.	Leaves assignments unfinished.
Writes down assignments when receiving them.	Doesn't write down assignments but tries to remember them.
Tries to do projects right the first time.	Must usually redo projects to correct mistakes.
Creates a schedule and tries to stick to it.	Follows no schedule for getting work done.
Knows how to say "no" to interruptions.	Allows self to be continuously distracted from work.
Starts projects as soon as possible and finishes them on time.	Procrastinates and regularly misses deadlines.
Commits self to a manageable number of projects.	Overcommits self and usually tries to do too much in too little time.
Uses small blocks of time creatively to accomplish work.	Wastes small blocks of time and accomplishes nothing.
Maintains an organized workplace.	Works in a disorganized mess.

EXERCISE

Do you practice self-discipline in your work? The answer is "yes" if you possess eight or more of the habits on the self-discipline chart. If not, you still have work to do.

"Self-discipline is a habit. And lack of it is a habit, too."

—Alec Mackenzie

Step 7: Monitor Your Progress

About a month ago, Roger had begun a program to organize his work more effectively. He was tired of feeling that his projects were controlling him, rather than the other way around. He regularly monitored his schedule to see where it seemed to be running smoothly and where he needed to make some changes. Roger discovered that he was still scheduling himself much too tightly. Almost every minute of the day was filled with some project. He never left time for a coffee break or lunch with friends.

(V. Harlow)

When you successfully complete a job, it's important to treat yourself to some time off. Arrange your schedule so you can spend part of each week just relaxing and recharging your batteries.

"Slack off a little," advises Lesley Alderman in *Money* magazine. "Squeeze some time into your schedule to simply chill out," Alderman adds. Roger never rewarded himself for a job well done; he just plunged into the next one. Roger needed to adjust his schedule to make it more flexible and less rigid.

Laura had the opposite problem. She would block out large chunks of time to handle different projects. But she would be easily distracted by handling unimportant telephone calls. After monitoring her schedule, Laura found that she was wasting an hour or more each night on these calls. Perhaps she needs more practice in learning how to say "no." She might also invest in an inexpensive answering machine to help her screen telephone calls, so she can deal with the unimportant ones later.

As you begin organizing your time, evaluate your schedule to determine how efficiently you are working. If you're driving yourself too hard, as Roger did, ease off a little bit. If you're distracted too easily, you may need to practice a little self discipline.

DEVELOP YOUR ORGANIZATION SKILLS

Developing your organization skills is like fine-tuning an engine. It takes some tinkering and adjustment. The seven secrets discussed in this chapter can help. Remember, it's important to be as realistic as possible. Don't overschedule yourself, and be sure to leave some time to pursue your personal goals, or just take it easy. You'll have more time if you put your schedule in writing so you don't have to keep trying to remember it. You'll also pick up valuable extra time if you store everything in its proper place so you don't have to search for it. Do assignments right the first time so they don't have to be done over.

None of these habits is easy—at least, not at first. They require self-discipline. But if you're prepared to monitor yourself regularly and keep making improvements, you will be successful.

GLOSSARY

In-box. A container on your desk for putting files and papers.

Perfectionism. A need to do every task perfectly, no matter how unimportant it may be.

Prioritize. To arrange in order of importance.

Procrastination. Constantly putting off tasks until the last minute.

Schedule. Organizing the items on your to-do list so they are accomplished in specific time periods.

Time management. A method of organizing each day so you accomplish your most important tasks.

Time wasters. Distractions that prevent you from doing your work.

To-do list. A list of projects that you need to do each day or each week.

BIBLIOGRAPHY

Barnes, Emilie. *Simply Organized: The Life You Always Searched for …but Were Too Cluttered to Find.* Eugene, OR: Harvest House Publishers, Inc., 1997.

Covey, Stephen. *The 7 Habits of Highly Effective People.* New York: Simon and Schuster, 1989.

Douglass, Merrill and Donna Douglass. *Manage Your Time, Manage Your Work, Manage Yourself.* New York: Amacom, 1980.

Fry, Ron. *Manage Your Time.* Danbury, CT: Grolier, 1991.

Griessman, B. Eugene. *Time Tactics of Very Successful People.* New York: McGraw Hill, 1994.

Kanarek, Lisa. *Everything's Organized.* Franklin Lakes, NJ: Career Press, Inc., 1996.

Lipnack, Jessica. *The Age of the Network: Organizing Principles for the 21st Century.* New York: John Wiley & Sons, Inc., 1995.

Livesay, Corinne R. *Getting & Staying Organized.* Des Moines, IA: American Media, Inc., 1996

Mackenzie, Alec. *The Time Trap.* New York: Amacom, 1990.

Mayer, Jeffrey. *Time Management for Dummies.* Foster City, CA: IDG Books, 1995.

National Association of Professional Organizers, San Francisco Bay Area Chapter Staff. *Organizing Options: Solutions from Professional Organizers.* San Francisco, CA: National Association of Professional Organizers.

Winston, Stephanie. *Getting Organized.* New York: Warner Books, 1990.

Winston, Stephanie. *The Organized Executive.* New York: Warner Books, 1994.